# The
# North York Moors
# In Old Postcards

## ARAF CHOHAN

There are many family and friends that have passed on, but some will always hold a special place in my heart and they are remembered here for having enriched my life, but for all too short a time.

A family member who is also a friend is one of the joys of human relationships. I was lucky to have had my favourite cousin Anwar Lal Bhadshah, who was also my best friend.

Those who have held special places in my heart and who were very, very dear to me include Baksh Allahi (Bodee), who was a loyal and caring friend. Also my British Airways friends, Betty Palmer and Julia Sherry. and the wonderful times I had with them which will be forever remembered and never forgotten.

**Copyright © 2015 Araf Chohan**

First Edition 2015
Published by Destinworld Publishing Ltd.
**www.destinworld.com**

British Library Cataloguing-in-Publication Data
A catalogue record for this book is available from the British Library.

ISBN 978 0 9930950 2 3

# ACKNOWLEDGEMENTS

All the postcard images contained within this publication come entirely from my own personal collection, so there remains only a few individuals whom I need to thank; those who have helped to bring this book to its final fruitful conclusion.

A special heartfelt thanks to Catherine Powloski, who way back in 1968 befriended a very young 15 year old, and especially in my very early years of postcard hunting in the capital gave me my own key to her London home. It was my true home away from home all those years ago.

In the years to follow there were many friends and family who were all supportive of my postcard collecting, but premier amongst them is my former British Airways colleague and close friend John Monaghan. For over 25 years John has given me shelter, help and support during my postcard collecting trips to London and the Home Counties. He continues to this day, always there for me on all my visits to London. He is a true and caring friend.

Of the many friends who have been supportive of my postcard collecting, I'd like to thank Mary and Michael Day. Having met them in 1969, they have stayed in touch and followed my life's journey.

A special mention of my dearest friends Laila Hitchens, Lulu, Waqas Butt, Gurmej Shina (my "second sister"), and not forgetting cousin Shah Nawaz, nephews Shah Heer and Khurram Ellahi.

Last but not least my caring nephew but a true friend Hamza Ellahi who has been constant in his support in all that I embark upon.

Matt Falcus has been instrumental in his encouragement, coupled with his patience, help and total support in bringing this North York Moors book to its final conclusion and publication via Destinworld.

Araf Chohan

# CONTENTS

# INTRODUCTION

This book is purely and simply a nostalgic look at the North York Moors and its immediate surroundings as seen in old picture postcards. In most pictures it reflects a time around a hundred years ago, when communication via the medium of sending postcards was at its zenith, and many thousands were sent annually between the late 1890's till the end of the Great War of 1914-18, after which the craze began to decline. The vast majority of the images here span this great Edwardian period, as well as the First World War era (essentially an extension of the period) plus some from later periods.

This was an elegant and colourful time, when Britain was at the height of its Empire and global power; a time when its people enjoyed their leisure time, be it by the seaside or the countryside, in a very sedate manner - compared to the fast pace of life today. As such, the pages of this book take the reader back in time to see the long-lost world of tranquil and rural Yorkshire, with its quaint villages and small market towns – in many cases representing a way of life that has now long gone.

The photographs speak for themselves. Therefore, I have kept the captions to a bare minimum, as I wish the reader to be an avid viewer, to delve into and enjoy the images of this distant time. This was a time when there was no television, let alone computers or mobile phones, and the automobile were not commonplace.

At the heart of North Yorkshire and its beautiful moorland is the North York Moors National Park, founded in 1952. It is one of the largest and most beautiful expanses of heather moorland in Britain, however it was not a National Park when these images were taken, beautiful and treasured as it was. The area then was without crowds and modern developments, but was still beautiful and a draw to visitors, as can be seen by the photos contained within.

North Yorkshire is the place of my birth and Middlesbrough, my home town, sits on the very edge of the North York Moors. Many a summer (plus the odd winter) I would be rambling, picnicking and simply enjoying a day out amongst family and friends in the glorious countryside, or beside the sea at Whitby, Staithes or Runswick Bay. Childhood memories abound, but as I still live just ten minutes away, I am a regular visitor to the Moors and seaside, just as before. The memories flood back to those times during the 1950s and 60s when I would be with my loving parents, brothers and sister on our family outings to Roseberry Topping, Captain Cook's Monument or the seaside at Saltburn, Marske or Whitby. It was a time for great enjoyment of simpler pleasures and a time of innocence. Above it all was the majesty and grandeur of the North York Moors, with all its glorious seasons full of colour and unsurpassed beauty, that I adore.

# WHITBY AND THE COAST

WHITBY FROM THE AIR

An impressive aerial view of Whitby gives visitors an impression of the site of the Abbey, St. Mary's Church, and the town beyond.

A 1930 view of the sands and promenades north of the harbour entrance at Whitby, with many bathers enjoying the beach.

The Front on Whitby's West Cliff. Visitors relax watching the view and taking the sea air. A father can be seen trying out the viewing telescope whilst his child waits on patiently.

The ruined Benedicting Whitby Abbey of St. Hilda on the wild clifftop has been a popular attraction for visitors to the town for centuries. It was founded in 657 and dissolved by King Henry VIII. Bram Stoker immortalised it in his Dracula novel, and it was significantly damaged by shelling during World War I.

Whitby Pavilion overlooks the West Cliff and Sands. It is a popular attraction even today, with magnificent views along the coast.

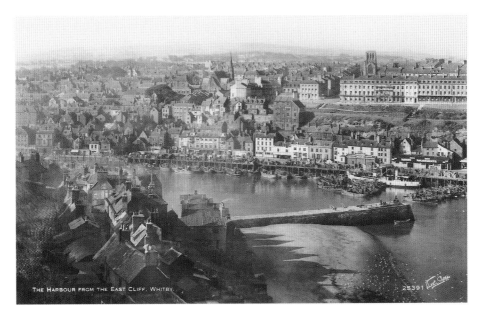

Looking down on the rows of fishing vessels in Whitby Harbour from the East Cliff. Amusements arcades have already made an appearance by this time, occupying the buildings lining the harbour.

Today much of Whitby Harbour has been reclaimed to create space to build a car park and other structures. However, this photograph shows what it was like when hundreds of fishing boats and other vessels crowded the harbour as part of a thriving industry which supported the town.

IT'S LOVELY ON WHITBY SANDS    FMS 268/2

The caption says it all! Whitby has long attracted holidaymakers to enjoy its beaches and the fine summer weather. The sand is particularly good for sandcastles!

The twin lighthouses at the ends of Whitby's harbour piers are a welcoming sight to seafarers in wild conditions. This painting depicts their beams shining bright on a rough night.

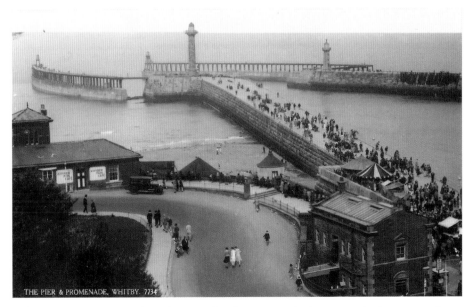

THE PIER & PROMENADE, WHITBY. 7734

With the twisting Kyber Pass in the foreground, the extended piers at the entrance to Whitby's harbour can be seen stretching beyond. Hundreds of visitors are enjoying a walk to the end, which has views along the coast.

No doubt sold to guests, this postcard shows an aerial view of the Metropole Hotel on Whitby's West Cliff. Built in the 1800s to cater for the thousands of visitors flocking to the resort every year, today the building has been converted into private and holiday apartments.

Whitby suffered a significant flood in May 1932, which was recorded on this postcard showing the Empire Theatre and Station Hotel with water flowing into their ground floors.

The current Whitby Harbour bridge was built in 1908 and opens to allow vessels to pass underneath, whilst connecting the older and newer parts of the town across the River Esk.

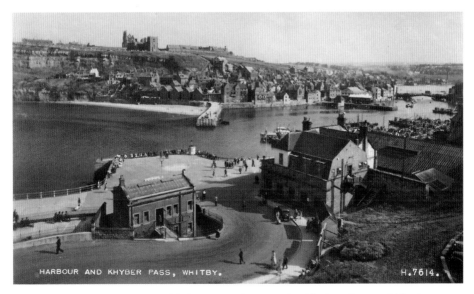

Named after the famous Afghan travel route, the Khyber Pass in Whitby is a twisting road leading from the harbour up the West Cliff. It was built in the 1850s when this area was developed for tourism.

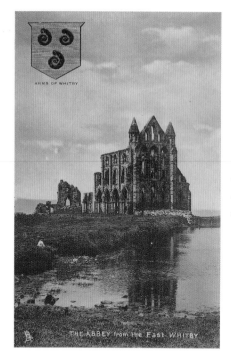

A classic view of the ruins of Whitby Abbey, facing west with the pond in the foreground. The card features the Arms of Whitby.

Another postcard to feature the Arms of Whitby, this time showing the East Cliff and entrance to the harbour.

A colourful painting of Whitby's Market Place in the old town.

The beach and harbour piers at Whitby feature in this early colour photograph.

Four attractive colour scenes of Whitby and the River Esk.

Whitby once had two railway stations, although only the larger exists today at the end of the Esk Valley line. Steam trains are just as common today as they were when this picture was taken thanks to the North Yorkshire Moors Railway which connects the town via Grosmont with its restored engines and carriages.

THE DINNER HOUR

Most seaside resorts along the North Yorkshire coast offered donkey rides along the sands to holidaymakers. This painting depicts the life of the boys who work the donkeys.

SANDSEND, looking WEST.                                    T.WATSON-LYTHE

Looking inland along Sandsend Beck. This painting is by T. Watson of Lythe - a village on the hill above Sandsend.

A lovely painting of Eastrow Beck in Sandsend, with children playing in the water and horses crossing.

Another painting of Sandsend, as seen from Mulgrave Woods and Dunsley Moor.

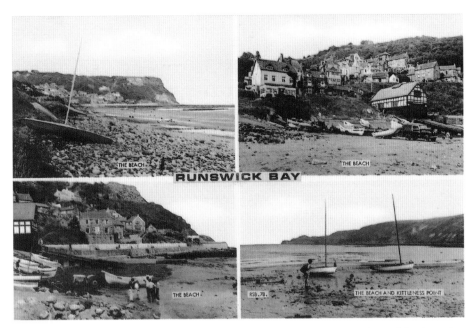

Five scenes of the beach at Runswick Bay, tinted in colour from black and white photographs.

The North Yorkshire coast is known for its fierce storms and wild seas. This postcard demonstrates what it can be like, especially in places like Runswick Bay which have been swept away and lost many lives to the sea in the past.

01003    THE BANK AND VILLAGE, RUNSWICK BAY

Visitors approaching Runswick Bay are often taken aback by the views over the sea, and the houses of the village huddled precariously on the cliff face. The twisting road climbing up behind the village has since been superseded by a much straighter, but no less steep, replacement.

Families enjoy an outing to Runswick Bay with its fine beach and sweeping views. Fishing boats are pulled up from the shore and the lifeboat station can be seen in the background.

Runswick Bay here in 1918 looks much the same as it does today, however life revolved much more around its fishing industry.

The village of Aislaby lies a couple of miles west of Whitby, overlooking the River Esk valley. Aislaby Hall was built in the 1800s and this postcard shows off its gardens.

*Ugthorpe Lodge. 1.* ∠*y*+*H*℔

Built as a hunting lodge in 1605, Ugthorpe Lodge is in Lythe, to the north of Whitby and Sandsend. Today it has been converted into a country hotel and pub.

WHITBY, RUNSWICK BAY

An artistically-coloured photograph of Runswick Bay from the turn of the last century, showing the village, beach and fishing boats.

This postcard clearly demonstrates the difficulties in constructing roads to villages on the Moors coast. Zig Zag Bank leads to Robin Hood's Bay, which can be seen in the background.

A colour tinted scene of Robin Hood's Bay paints a sunny and attractive picture to send to loved ones at home.

An old view of the narrow New Road shortly before the buildings open up to the sea beyond. It shows the busy life of a fishing village at the time.

A worker and his horses on the sands at Robin Hood's Bay make an attractive scene.

*St. Stephen's Church, Robin Hood's Bay*

St. Stephen's Church near Robin Hood's Bay was built between 1868 and 1870. This photograph was taken in 1905 and shows its uniquely shaped tower and large nave. It replaced Old St. Stephen's Church, which is a smaller structure that still stands today.

RAVENSCAR - STATION

Formerly known as The Peak, Ravenscar Station was opened in 1885 on the Scarborough & Whitby Railway. It was originally planned to build a holiday resort next to the village, with streets and sewers being laid out. But no more than a few houses were ever built.

Steps built alongside the steep road passing through Robin Hood's Bay aid pedestrians walking through the village, which straddles the side of the bank.

Looking over the narrow river gorge and the town of Staithes with its harbour and the North Sea beyond. A young James Cook worked as an apprentice here before going on to greater adventures at Whitby.

An early example of a resort built to house holidaymakers to the Yorkshire coast at The Holiday Fellowship near Staithes. This card was posted in 1937.

A group of ladies pose at the top of the steps leading to a narrow wynd. In the distance, the Cod and Lobster public house can be seen.

The foreshore at Staithes in the early 1940s, before the harbour wall was built to provide safe shelter to boats from the often wild North Sea.

The little fishing town of Staithes lies on the banks of a deep creek through which the Roxby Beck flows to the sea.

Staintondale is a small village near Ravenscar which was on the Scarborough & Whitby railway line. It can be seen passing under the road bridge at the bottom of this card, whilst a typical Moors vista extends to the horizon.

# GOATHLAND AND THE ESK VALLEY

This 1911 postcard is a painting by Tom Bogus showing the Moorland Road near Goathland, with a standing stone and signpost so typical of the area.

A steam train powers through Pernholme near Goathland on the Whitby and Pickering Railway in the 1940s. This line would close in 1965, but reopen for tourists in 1973.

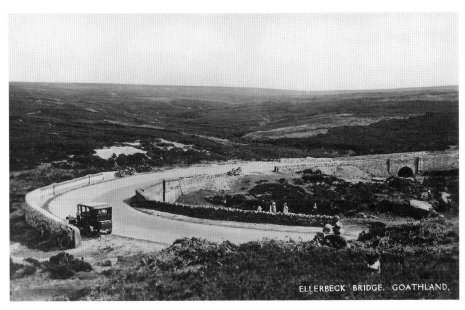

Motorists and cyclists enjoy the open moors near Goathland. Eller Beck Bridge is still in use on the main road here today.

Although a black and white image, it is clear in this 1930s photograph that the sun is shining. The presence of a bus and cars parked on the grass indicates that tourism was already flourishing here.

This 1914 photograph of Goathland shows the active railway station at the bottom, which is now a part of the North Yorkshire Moors Railway.

Two men pose outside "Siding Cottage" in Beckhole, near Goathland. This card was posted in 1906.

A colour tinted scene of Goathland with sheep grazing alongside the main road through the village.

This scene near Goathland shows the vast open spaces and emptiness across the Moors.

A postcard of the small village of Beckhole near Goathland. The spelling often changes, depicted here as 'Bickhole'.

The pub in Beckhole is still a popular spot for weary walkers and motorists to stop for refreshment.

Another scene of the small community of Beckhole hidden in the valley of the Eller Beck.

Two men pose on the famous Beggar's Bridge in Glaisdale in the early 1900s.

Beggar's Bridge has always been a favourite spot to visit, but for much of its life was a main roadway over the River Esk.

A 1907 colour tinted postcard of the Horse Shoe Hotel in Egton Bridge.

Another card from Egton Bridge, this time showing the Station Hotel & Terrace.

BAY HORSE INN & GENERAL VIEW, LITTLEBECK.

Littlebeck is a tiny community near Sleights. Today the Bay Horse Inn is a private residence.

LEALHOLME BRIDGE. NO. 840.

A crowd poses on the bridge over the River Esk in Lealholm, with the village's Catholic Church in the background. This card was posted in 1917.

Many will be familiar with this row of cottages which are today home to the Moors National Park Centre at Danby. In this photograph they are still very much separate and private.

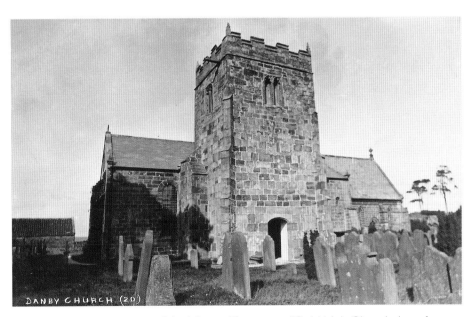

Danby is an ancient part of the Moors. The tower of St. Hilda's Church dates from the 15th century, with a more recent Victorian rebuild of the nave and chancel.

This picture is a reminder of the rural life which underpins the North York Moors, and which attracted many early tourists to the area.

The main road through the Esk Valley was much quieter when this was a remote rural area compared to today.

DANBY, DUCK'S BRIDGE.                    Nº829.

The single arched 14th century Duck's Bridge near Danby Castle was still in use at the time of this early colour tinted picture postcard. Today pedestrians can still walk across it.

RUSWARP, BOAT LANDING.                   Nº856.

Boats line the shore awaiting tourists and locals to hire them for a trip on the River Esk as it widens near the coast.

A prime refreshments stop before climbing Blue Bank in Sleights, near Whitby, makes good use of passing travellers.

A 1912 postcard looking down into Sleights which was a much smaller village than it is today.

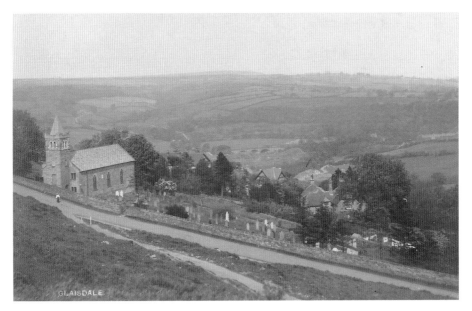

Looking down into the Esk Valley and St. Thomas' Church in Glaisdale.

The dramatic setting of the Moors is evident in this picture postcard of Glaisdale in the Esk Valley.

The Station Hotel in Castleton, with steps leading up to the station platform in the background.

The main road through Castleton in 1913 with many children present and a crowd in the distance.

Horses and carts rule the road, but in the background the railway station and industrial workings are clearly evident in this postcard of Castleton.

A view of Castleton and its parish church from the east of the village. This card was posted in 1938.

Castleton Moors in the Esk Valley depicted in an evocative painting showing the wild heather moorland and sheep farmer.

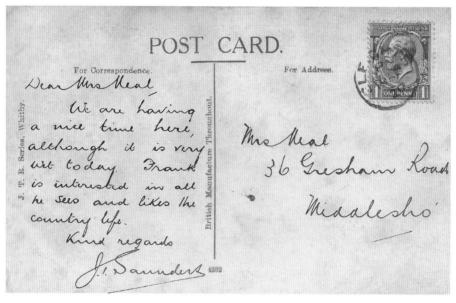

Like today, messages sent on cards often reflect on the weather and pace of life experienced on a holiday.

The railway in Grosmont has always been important. This scene shows the muddy main road passing over the level crossing with a number of public houses lining the steep road rising beyond.

# NORTHERN AND WESTERN MOORS

Roseberry Topping's unique shape dominates the view behind the nearby village of Roseberry Under Newton, with its Kings Head Hotel.

Great Ayton has been a draw for tourists for a long time. This multi-view card from 1935 shows some of the main attractions of the village.

A later 1958 view of Waterfall Terrace in Great Ayton.

Looking recently built, as the name suggests, is New Bridge in the centre of Great Ayton. It carries the main road through the village.

Motor cars and bicycles parked outside the shops of High Green in Great Ayton.

THE SCHOOL AT GREAT AYTON WHERE JAMES COOK WAS EDUCATED.
THE STAIRCASE LEADS TO THE SCHOOLROOM, NOW A MUSEUM.
"TEESSIDE MUSEUMS AND ART GALLERIES" SERVICE.

Great Ayton's former schoolroom, where James Cook was educated, which had already been turned into a museum when this picture was taken.

AIREYHOLME FARM, NEAR GREAT AYTON. WHERE JAMES COOK,
AS A BOY, WORKED WITH HIS FATHER.
"TEESSIDE MUSEUMS AND ART GALLERIES" SERVICE.

Much of Great Ayton's fame comes from being home to the young James Cook. He lived and worked at Aireyholme Farm, near Roseberry Topping.

Seven black and white scenes from Captain Cook's life, including his birthplace and memorials in nearby Marton and on top of Easby Hill. This card marks the bi-centenary of his birth in 1928.

Three scenes of Captain Cook's life, in Marton (now part of Middlesbrough), Whitby, and the memorial on Easby Hill.

CAPTAIN COOK'S MONUMENT ON EASBY HILL
(CLEVELAND). NO. 1397.

The impressive obelisk to mark the life of Captain James Cook can be seen for miles around atop Easby Hill on the western flank of the North York Moors.

Roseberry, Newton                                                    4994

The dorsal fin of Roseberry Topping stands at almost 1,050ft. When this picture was taken many in the village of Newton would remember its more conical shape before a partial collapse in 1912.

Little Ayton is the smaller village near Great Ayton on the north western side of the Moors.

The Black Horse public house and houses in Newlands, Great Broughton, around 1914.

Walkers pose on the quiet Grange Avenue in Great Broughton. This card was posted in 1909.

The unusual shapes of the Wainstones on Hasty Bank above Great Broughton make an interesting collection of pictures on this postcard.

Three tinted photographs from Great Broughton, showing the housing and agriculture of the village.

An early 1906 colour tinted card of the Post Office and Institute at Hutton Rudby on the edge of the Moors.

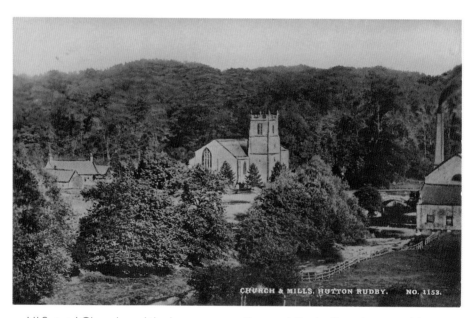

All Saints' Church and the long-gone mills straddle the River Leven in Hutton Rudby.

Built in 1838 for the daughter of King William IV and her husband, Skutterskelf Hall is known today as Rudby Hall.

A snowy winter scene in Hutton Rudby reproduced as a postcard by Stevens of Thirsk.

East Harlsey is a small village in the shadow of the Hambleton Hills on the western edge of the Moors.

The Post Office and centre of Kirby-in-Cleveland, a small village on the west of the Moors.

A leafy country lane leading down to Swainby must have painted an idyllic scene of the area when folks back home received this postcard.

Various views of Swainby and nearby Whorlton, showing both churches and the popular Scugdale Beck passing through.

The road leading to Whorlton, with Holy Cross Church in the background.
This colour tinted photograph dates from 1911.

Swainby is a village on the north-western corner of the North York Moors.
Much of its growth occurred when housing was needed for miners, but it has
remained very picturesque, as seen here.

Examples of the houses built for miners in Swainby in the 19th century still make a good subject for a postcard.

Older than Swainby is the parish church of Whorlton, located close to the ruins of the castle of the same name. It is the site of an older deserted village.

Mount Grace Priory was of the Carthusian Order. It fell into disrepair following dissolution in 1539.

The 13th Century manor house at Mount Grace Priory, hiding the ruins of the monastery beyond.

OSMOTHERLEY "SCARTH NICK" FROM SHEEP WASH BECK BANK.    NO. 1534

Sheep Wash near Osmotherley looks bleak and remote in this black and white postcard, but is known today as a popular spot to visit on the Moors.

The Valley Pool, Osmotherley

The quiet Valley Pool near Osmotherley in 1936.

This card, posted in 1909, shows the Chequers Inn on the drover's road near Osmotherley. The building is a private house today.

This cosy interior of the Chequers Inn, where the fire had reputedly burned for over 200 years.

Groceries, Teas and Provisions of the Finest Quality

**EDWARD D. THOMPSON, Grocer, Draper, & Newsagent, Osmotherley.** *Established 1800*

Thompson's shop has been a landmark in Osmotherley since 1800. No doubt it produced this postcard to sell to customers.

A child stands outside a cottage in the otherwise deserted village of Osmotherley.

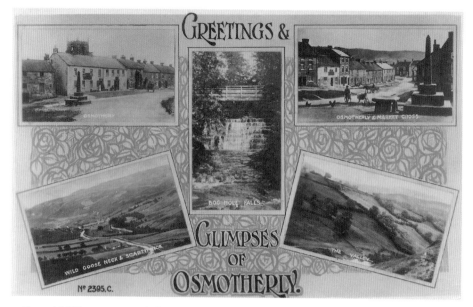

Five 1920s scenes of Osmotherley and the surrounding area in a card intended for visitors to send to those back home.

This colour tinted photograph of the centre of Osmotherley shows Thompson's store and the Golden Lion pub.

A quiet day in Osmotherley, with two people posing in the foreground, and various goods stacked outside the shop in the distance.

Osmotherley from Ruebury.

An overview of the village of Osmotherley from Ruebury.

The signpost helps place this village of Hawnby, seen here around 1920.

The Buck Inn at Chop Gate (pronounced Chop Yat) in Bilsdale has been a convenient watering hole and inn for many years.

The Blackwell Ox public house is just visible through the trees behind the horse and cart in this view of Carlton.

Dating from the 1700s, Busby Hall lies hidden in woodland close to Carlton-in-Cleveland.

An attractive sunny scene created from a black and white photograph, looking towards the Cleveland Hills.

St. Botolph's Church sits just inside the present day National Park in the village of Carlton-in-Cleveland.

Children have been assembled in their finest clothes in front of the Manor House in Carlton-in-Cleveland for this attractive postcard.

The village of Faceby sits in the shadow of the Cleveland Hills on the western edge of the National Park.

An original farmhouse and the bleak Moors beyond provide a contrast to the new terraced houses built at Charltons, near Guisborough.

Like Margrove Park, Charltons appeared suddenly on the edge of the Moors when workers were needed for the nearby mines. Its rows of terraced houses provided substantial accommodation.

Battersby grew into an important village at the head of the Esk Valley leading into the Moors. Its station connected two different railway lines, and the impressive Incline led trains up the side of the hills towards the mines of Rosedale.

The North Yorkshire & Cleveland Railway reached Ingleby on 1st February 1858. The line was laid with double track and the station included both up and down platforms.

No 342.    NEWGATE WOOD, BILSDALE.

A lone cyclist travels through Newgate Wood in Bilsdale in the western Moors.

Close to the northern edge of the North York Moors, shop keepers and residents pose in Lingdale's main street for a postcard that was probably sold in one of the shops seen here.

The village of Margrove Park appeared on the site of a former deer park near Charltons. It was established to house workers from the nearby mine. Most of the houses were demolished following the mine's closure in 1924.

The busy centre of Stokesley, a short distance from the edge of the North York Moors. It is one of the great market towns of the area.

Many travellers on the A19 will recognise this landmark which is now a hotel and restaurant. In this view the building was still a private residence known as Ingleby House.

This unique and tiny church in Upleatham is one of the smallest in the country. It was once part of a much larger building.

Loftus dates from the 7th Century, but much of it today reflects the boom in the mining industry in more recent years. It is situated on the very edge of what is today the National Park.

Five scenes of the busy market town of Northallerton, showing the Market Place, County Hall, South Parade, Parish Church and Market Cross.

Like many great Yorkshire towns, Northallerton's Market Place is set in a wide High Street where traders' stalls and vehicles can be set up to attract passing traffic. This photograph is from 1941.

Sowerby's Parish Church dates from around 1140, although it was rebuilt in 1842. Today the village is very much a part of Thirsk.

Looking down towards Thirsk from Plump Bank in a time when roads were often empty of any form of traffic.

Sutton-under-Whitestonecliff is a village underneath one of the most spectacular parts of the North York Moors. The view from the top of the cliff beyond is stunning, and many travellers will have passed along this road before ascending the steep gradient.

Thirsk's busy railway station looking north.

Romanby is a small village situated alongside Northallerton to the west of the North York Moors.

This photograph of New County Hall was posted in 1908, and presumably taken to show off the grand new building which was opened two years earlier.

# THE SOUTHERN MOORS

The pretty village of Lastingham as seen from the cross which overlooks it on the hill above. This is a popular vantage point and way marker for walkers even today.

Lastingham as seen in 1942. When much of Europe was suffering the ravages of war, a visitor was still able to send this tranquil scene to those at home.

A relatively unknown village, Lastingham is the site of an early monastery where the current stone church sits.

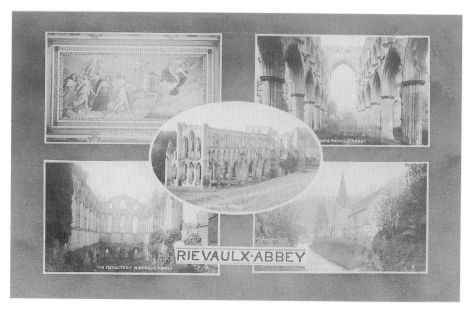

Five different scenes from around Rievaulx and its abbey.

One of the cottages in the secluded village of Rievaulx operated as a post office for many years, and no doubt sold this postcard. Today it is a private residence.

The towering ruins of the chancel and nave of Rievaulx Abbey near Helmsley.

The impressive and ruined Cistercian Rievaulx Abbey has been a draw for tourists for a long time. Part of its charm is the scale of the buildings which are hidden away in an almost secret valley.

Farmers pose on Castlegate in Helmsley with a team of Oxen pulling their cart.

A hunt gathers on Helmsley Market Place in front of the Black Swan Hotel.

The towering East Tower of Helmsley Castle with sheep grazing around. The castle was still a private residence until the early 1700s when nearby Duncombe Park was built. Today it is in the care of English Heritage and is a popular tourist attraction.

One of the gateways in the walls of Helmsley Castle which were ordered destroyed by Parliament during the English Civil War. Once the castle was left to ruin, sheep began grazing in the remains until it was opened as a tourist attraction.

A colourful scene of pedestrians and residents on Helmsley's Castlegate, leading up to the church, in fine weather.

A 1950s postcard of the Market Place in Helmsley. Cars have now started to dominate the roads compared with earlier scenes.

Duncombe Park was built in the early 1700s to replace Helmsley Castle as a home for Thomas Brown (later Duncombe). It sits in 300 acres of land around the River Rye, to the south of the town.

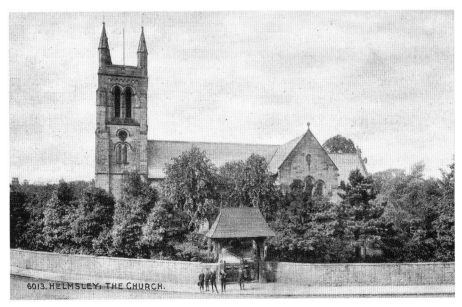

All Saints' Church contains much stonework from its Norman construction, although it has been restored and altered a number of times. It became a listed building in 1955, but is seen in this postcard around 40 years earlier.

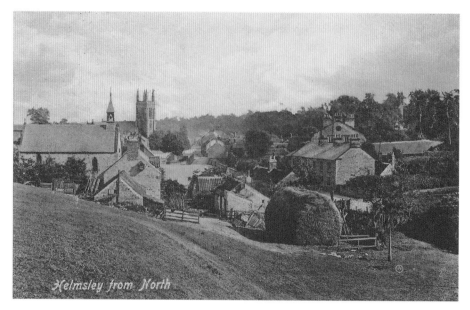

Looking over the rooftops of Helmsley in 1912, with the tower of All Saints' Church visible in the background, and part of the castle in the trees to the right.

High Street in Helmsley, with a mixture of horse and cart and motor vehicle traffic along High Street. The presence of a speed limit sign demonstrates how the use of cars must have been growing at the time of the photograph.

A horse and cart travels towards Helmsley's Market Place along Bondgate, which leads out of the town to the east. This card was sent in 1907.

The sender of this postcard reflected on the glorious weather and local scenery experienced in and around Helmsley. The High Street certainly offers a similar scene today, albeit with much more road and pedestrian traffic.

Established in 1668, the Bilsdale Hunt is the oldest in England. It would often operate through Helmsley, no doubt stopping at the Black Swan Hotel for refreshment along the way.

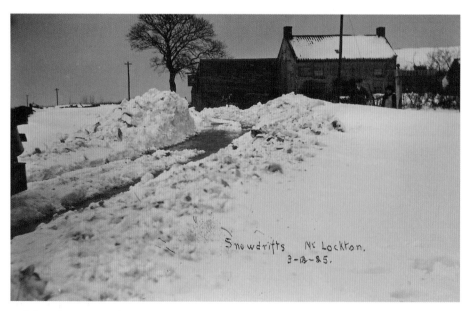

A family pose in the impressive snow drifts at Lockton in 1925, as described in the scratched-in annotation on this personal card.

One of a number of postcard scenes from Lockton in 1931. Visible in the distance is an early motor bus.

Farmers allow their weary horse to drink from the pond in the village whilst some ducks watch on. Another man looks curiously at the photographer capturing the scene.

Byland Abbey is one of the more distinctive ruined abbeys in the area, with the remains of its huge rose window pointing towards the sky. It was dissolved in 1538, sone 370 years before this colour tinted postcard was sent.

Ampleforth College hugs the southern boundary of the North York Moors. It is an impressive boarding school, founded in 1802 by the Benedictine monks of Ampleforth Abbey.

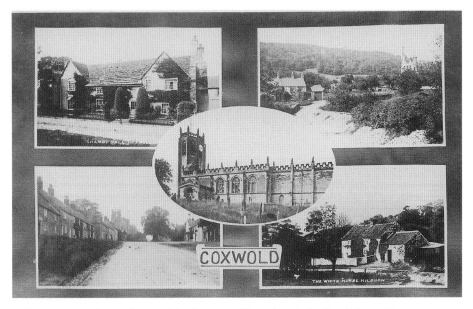

Five scenes from Coxwold, showing Shandy Hall, the White Horse near Kilburn, Byland Abbey, the parish church and the village.

An attractive tinted photograph of Kilburn, near Coxwold, with the Moors rising in the background.

A nicely framed postcard showing Kilburn's White Horse above the village and grazing sheep.

Just discernible on the hillside in the distance is the white horse which overlooks the village of Kilburn. It was created in 1857 and is visible from miles around.

An elegantly dressed lady looks over the scenic village of Hutton-le-Hole. This card was posted in 1903.

Pickering Beck is prone to regular flooding. Here children make the most of
a particularly bad flood in 1927 to row down the Market Place.

Newton Dale to the north of Pickering carries the line of what is today the
North Yorkshire Moors Railway towards Goathland, Grosmont and Whitby.

Children and passers-by watch Pickering Beck flow beneath the four-arched road bridge. Pickering Station can be seen in the background.

A 1920 interior photograph of Pickering's Anglican church.

A series of paintings adorn the walls of Pickering Church, depicting scenes and inspiration from the Bible and the Martyrdom of Saint Tomas Becket. These scenes were covered up for centuries until being restored in 1867. This selection of postcards show off the scenes and made a nice collector's set.

The approach into Pickering from Scarborough. As well as the horse and cart and children, a policeman is also visible in this picture.

Pickering's ruinous 13th century castle sits high above the town and has been an important attraction for visitors to the town.

The secluded Douthwaite Dale near Kirkbymoorside demonstrates the peace and scenery of this part of the world. This card was posted in 1925 to family in London.

Castlegate, looking downhill into Kirkbymoorside, as seen in 1912.

As its name suggests, Railway Street once led to Kirkbymoorside's railway station. However, following its closure in 1964, the street is now known as Piercy End.

A busy scene from the 1940s is captured in this postcard, with early motorcars and a cattle market taking place.

Kirkbymoorside sits on the plain beneath the Moors. This early photograph shows the contrast between the rural and urban areas.

Ladies in elegant dresses and shopkeepers displaying their goods in an otherwise quiet scene from Kirkbymoorside.

Thornton Dale.

A horse and cart is led along Chestnut Avenue in Thornton-le-Dale where it follows the path of Thornton Beck. Today this is the busy main road through the village.

THORNTON LE DALE

The lack of cars makes this scene hard to date, but it is certainly of a quieter time than today in this popular tourist village.

The Village, Rosedale Abbey.—          FRITH RSBY. 20

Named after a long-gone Cistercian priory of the same name, Rosedale Abbey is a pretty village in the southern Moors with a number of small tea shops and lodgings. This colour tinted card was posted in 1969, but is likely a little older than that since colour photographs were already being used at this time. It nevertheless paints a sunny scene found by so many visitors to what was by now a National Park.

# SCARBOROUGH AND SURROUNDINGS

This tinted photograph could almost be a painting, showing Scarborough lighthouse. It was posted to a family in the south in 1907.

The impressive sweep of Scarborough's South Bay as seen from the castle walls. The cramped houses and premises of Quay Street can clearly be seen in the foreground.

When this photograph was taken of the Italian Gardens in Scarborough they would have been newly opened. Visitors marvel at the pond and statue in the tranquil setting.

SOUTH BAY, SCARBOROUGH BY NIGHT

799

A wonderful, sweeping view of Scarborough at night, with the castle lit up in the distance. In the foreground a crowd has gathered to watch musicians on the bandstand near the spa.

533 Scarborough - South Sands

Posted in 1929, this postcard shows a wealth of life on the South Sands. Bathers were a lot more conservative in their beachwear compared to today!

This colour tinted photograph could almost be a painting. The elegant façade of Scarborough Railway Station can be seen, with trams running along Westborough and a hint of the castle in the background.

Crowds gather around the bathing pool built into the seashore whilst a brave few paddle in its waters. This scene is a perfect reflection of the importance of Scarborough as a holiday resort, with hundreds of people visible as far as the eye can see.

Scarborough was one of the first places in the country to be attacked during World War I by the German Navy. As this postcard commemorates, the bombardment took place on 16th December, 1914.

This shop on Prospect Road suffered the loss of one person inside during the surprise bombardment of Scarborough.

A 1930s scene of the harbour. Busy pleasure boats share the pier with working vessels, and a row of cars from the era can be seen parked. In the background visitors can be seen walking up Castle Hill.

Bathing tents litter the beach at nearby Filey to protect the modesty of those who wish to bathe or relax.

These bungalows were built to house visitors and bathers to the quieter North Sands beach, but have all since been demolished to allow a road and car parking to be installed.

The Bowling Green in Alexandra Gardens in the northern part of Scarborough. Gentlemen dressed appropriately for the game, whilst women and children watched on. This card was sent in 1928.

Tourists lucky enough to find a seat on the veranda to the left of this scene look on in bemusement at the sheer chaos of thousands of people crowding the Foreshore and trams during the busy summer season in Scarborough.

Eastborough is one of Scarborough's busiest thoroughfares, and seen here with shops, pubs, a hotel and many early motor vehicles.

Church Stairs Street still exists today, but these cottages and houses are long gone. The street leads to St. Mary's Church on top of the hill.

The promenade is lit up and the waves and bare trees suggest this is a winter scene along South Bay, with The Spa and bandstand in the foreground.

PAGEANT OF THE BOHEMIAN GIRL, OPEN AIR THEATRE, SCARBOROUGH    1983

The Open Air Theatre in Northstead Manor Gardens has a magical setting next to the lake, with the castle as a backdrop. It has attracted crowds for performances on summer evenings since it opened in 1932.

A lone tram glides down the bank into the Ramsdale Valley, behind the Esplanade.

A single decker tram sweeps round the corner and up Vernon Road in front of Scarborough Museum and Aquarium in the Ramsdale Valley. Dominating the skyline is the Grand Hotel.

A colour 1960s photograph of the harbour taken from the lighthouse. It is interesting to contrast this with the earlier picture of the same area on page 116 in the 1930s.

A more recent colour photograph of the harbour brings the seaside location to life.

Seen here shortly after its opening in 1921 is the magnificent Futurist theatre and cinema, which stands on Foreshore Road, fronting South Bay. The building still exists, but closed as a cinema in 2014.

Another view of Scarborough's Italian Gardens with elegantly dressed visitors enjoying the fine weather.

THE STATION, SCALBY.

Scalby Station on the outskirts of Scarborough had an ivy-covered bridge at the end of the platform which seemed to whisk trains out of nowhere towards the platform. The station and line, which led to Whitby West Cliff, were demolished in the 1960s.

BURNISTON.

Burniston is a small village to the north of Scarborough on the main road to Whitby. In this 1915 photograph it is still very much an agricultural community.

Five scenes of Scarborough, tinted to advertise the blue skies and waters to be found here.

A smart painting of the Royal Hotel on Scarborough's sea front, no doubt commissioned to sell to tourists and guests visiting the town.